❝ Your story is a jewel, it is an unpretentious, yet very subtle mountain of wisdom. Or is it simply an accumulation of neatly and eloquently phrased common-sense?

'Book' in my view is not the right label. It is more of a new companion, a new found friend that you can enjoy listening to, and whilst listening (i.e. reading), you almost feel the urge to start talking to him, to share your feelings, reaction, excitement and experiences with him, in ever growing waves of recognition and curiosity. ❞

~ RvL (Zurich)

...and then *you're dead!*
47 reasons to start living your life...

Jim Rai

B L O O M S B U R Y
NEW DELHI • LONDON • OXFORD • NEW YORK • SYDNEY

First Published, 2015

BLOOMSBURY PUBLISHING INDIA PVT. LTD.
New Delhi London Oxford New York Sydney

ISBN: 978-93-85436-73-4

10 9 8 7 6 5 4 3 2 1

Published by Bloomsbury Publishing India Pvt. Ltd.
DDA Complex LSC, Building No. 4, 2nd Floor
Pocket 6 & 7, Sector C
Vasant Kunj, New Delhi 110070

Published in the United Kingdom by Compass Publishing, 2013

Set by The Book Refinery Ltd
Cover Design Smart Soho

Printed at Sanat Printers, Kundli, Sonipat, Haryana

Dedication

In the same year as this book was published, my Grandmother who reached the record-breaking age of 115, passed away peacefully in her sleep. She led an incredible life, which despite being filled with tragedy and challenges, she lived to the full. Sadly, all her children passed away before her eyes, including my mother, who died very young. At the age of 74, my Grandmother was left with the responsibility of raising her grandchildren.

This book is dedicated to these two truly amazing women who have been my inspiration, hope and belief, who have been with me throughout my journey
both in body and soul.

Contents

Introduction

It will come to us all, and then one fine day you are no more and this short journey on planet earth is over!

So I often ask myself, why do we speed up the process whilst we are still here?

If there is one eternal truth in this world (apart from taxes), it's that we will all come to the end of our life at some point. However, so many of us are simply trying to get through our day rather than living it. It has been said by many, that the real tragedy in this world is not death, but what we let die inside of us whilst we are still living. Are we living with our eyes open or closed? Are we really enjoying the life we have been given or simply just ticking the boxes as each year goes by?

Before we get to our day of truth, if I could ask for 90 minutes of your time (which is the average time of six coffee breaks for some), to reflect on where you are today, what your journey has been like so far and what lies ahead.

My name is Jim Rai; I have been with my partner for 27 years and she has given me four loving children. For the last 22 years of my working life, I have been living, what I call, a life of maintenance - getting to work, paying the bills and maintaining everything around me including the cushion covers. Without realising it, I had found myself simply ticking the boxes of existence and just trying to get through one year after the next - when finally I thought - STOP! WHAT ARE YOU DOING?

The reality is, that this book was conceived during a time in my life when I found it difficult to see where the light would come in from. I felt there had to be more. There had to be a way in which I could weave together my everyday living and the wisdom I had learnt along the way. With so much I had been meaning to say, but never quite had the time or the courage to do so, I put pen to paper.

Once I got typing, I felt a sense of freedom by expressing my thoughts. I was surprised at exactly how much my subconscious mind had absorbed over the years, and how much of it, in reality I was actually practising. Don't get me wrong, I have had a great life, but deep down in my heart I know it could have been way better.

Looking back now, I can see that many of us don't come up for air; we move around so fast in our action-packed lives and we're rarely still enough for long enough, to ask ourselves about our journey and where it's heading. When we do, we are either six feet underground or placed in an urn - which no doubt, you will have worked out, is slightly too late.

So, through these reflections, I hope you will take stock, and question where you are in your journey. If you feel a change is needed to improve the quality and outlook of your life, then I believe this book can assist. If there is just one lesson out of the 47 that I share, that creates a positive impact in your life, then this book was worth the time. I have tried to be practical, by building in realistic steps that you can incorporate into your daily routine without expecting a significant behaviour change overnight.

As they say, the smallest adjustment of the sail can send us on a completely different course.

I am no expert in the field of psychology; I'm just someone who was fortunate enough to spend time in the company of humble, wise and loving people who, through their actions, gave me an incredible education steeped in common sense and practicality.

So I very much hope that along with my children, you may find something in here that may improve and help make your life that little bit better each day. Certainly, what I have come to realise over time is that the answer to improving the quality of one's life, lies in its simplicity. I hope I have managed to capture the essence of this in the following pages.

Enjoy...

Take good care of your *knees.*

1

How many summers do you have left to go? Take a guess...

Don't take life so seriously as we are only visitors here
for a short time.

How many summers do you have left?

How many more times will you experience sitting outside during a summer evening, feel the sunshine warming your face, and that glowing feeling that actually the world can be a wonderful place when you see it in all its beauty, as the sun sets and rises.

I will be 47 years old by the time this collection of thoughts is published, and if I am lucky, I will possibly have 33 summers left to enjoy (the average life expectancy rate in the UK being 80). Not many really, when you think about it.

The real sadness is that when some of us do eventually come to realise that we only have a limited amount of summers left in us, we still don't make the most of them. So, please make the ones left count! You will not regret it – I promise!

Equally important to remember is that we are mere travellers passing through time, and that our journey is best measured by the strength and quality of the relationships we form along the way, rather than the reward miles we collect. To bring the point home, my father once explained to me that life was like a train journey, which starts with you inside a carriage with two people already there. Along the way, the train will stop at many stations allowing passengers to get in and out of your carriage. The secret is to try and enjoy their company, whilst trying to learn as much as possible from them as you can. There will be some people who may stay for only a stop, and you wish they had stayed for the entire journey. There will be others who stay for longer, but you wish they had only stayed for one stop.

It is important that while you enjoy your time with those in your carriage, you don't forget to keep looking out of your window and admire the view as the world is a beautiful place. At some point, you too will need to leave the train, as your journey will have come to an end, so enjoy the view and the company while you still can.

Do not judge by appearances. A rich heart may be under a poor coat, and the same can also apply the other way round.

2

Two categories of people – which one do you fall into?

If you had a choice, would you choose to be a person who is known for their positive outlook to life or for their negative one?

Which one do you fall into?

I once read about a man who was curious to find out what life was all about from those who had experienced it. He carried out a 20-year survey of all the retirement homes the full length and breadth of his country. His findings were quite simple. Having interviewed thousands of elderly people who had lived their lives, he concluded that ultimately there were two types of people in this world; there were those who were content with the life that they had lived and those that weren't, despite the fact that both these sets of people had experienced similar life circumstances throughout.

What does this tell you?

Well, it's all about your perspective, expectation and your attitude towards dealing with your individual circumstances. One set of people decided to embrace their problems and get on with life with a positive disposition; whilst the other got weighed down with them, blaming everyone for the difficulties they faced, and lived their entire lives with this attitude.

Interesting don't you think?

So, which category do you fall into?

(a) An optimistic (positive) person who says:

- *"Life is too short, so you should make the most of it."*

- *"Life is a journey, so enjoy the ride."*

- *"Remember, the glass is always half full."*

- *"Seize the day!"*

Or

(b) A pessimistic (negative) person who says:

- *"It's easier said than done."*

- *"I've heard it all before."*

- *"You're not being practical, this is the real world."*

- *"Who is going to pay my bills whilst I start thinking positive – you?"*

Take a minute and think about the answer.

Think about all the key choices you have made in your life and why you made them. Think about the attitude you regularly adopt to most situations. Think about your relationships with your partner, family and friends. Do you inspire others or do you drain them?

Do you look to find a solution or do you constantly dig up the past to perform the same examination time and time again?

The reality is, some people take the maximum out of life despite their problems, whilst others let their problems run their lives.

I believe that most people wish to be in the first category, but don't know how to get there.

Hopefully, this book will lend some perspective on how to achieve this.

One of my favourite sayings is, "*Our greatest danger in life, is not that our aim is too high, and we miss it but that it is too low and we reach it.*" **~ Michelangelo.**

...and guess what?

The answer to my opening line is – yes, you do in fact, have a choice, you just need the realisation that it all comes down to *you making it!*

Dear Optimist, Pessimist * *and Realist,*
While you guys were busy arguing about the glass of water, I drank it!
Sincerely,
The Opportunist.

3

The 70% rule

*Try to aim for at least a 70% positive day by adopting a
forward–looking and confident attitude to your life and
relationships. However, do not beat yourself up over it if you don't
quite get there, after all you are human, and all human beings
have some negative thoughts and times of indecision.*

Why 70%?

Call it a gut feeling (or if it makes you feel better, let us pretend it is
based on years of scientific research), anything more than 70% is
unrealistic, anything less is not making the most of your day.

At times, we all suffer from bouts of anger, frustration, sadness, irritation
and feeling low, which is perfectly normal. Being positive and keeping
the 70% philosophy in mind, doesn't mean you will avoid negative
moments, just that you will reduce the amount of time you feel that
way. You see, the point here, is that your entire life and how you live it,
is in fact, a reflection of your everyday experiences and feelings.

The idea is to build the 70% rule into your psyche, ingrain it into your subconscious mind, and make the majority of your day a positive, progressive one. Doing this will ensure that only a minimum part of your day is in the negative zone.

Too often, I see an imbalance in the equation, with people getting sucked into their work lives, trying to make it to the end of the day. They then tend to use short-term fixes (such as alcohol), to help alleviate themselves from its stresses and chase an artificial happiness, which is at best, momentary.

The 70% rule will help create a better environment throughout your day and more importantly, throughout your life.

Learn to continually absorb the 70% rule into your subconscious mind and it will slowly become an intrinsic part of you.

If you don't ask, then the answer is always "no!"

4

Too much thinking – relax!

Stop thinking too much and too deeply, you will run yourself into the ground! Not all questions have an answer, move on!

Move on!

The unknown has a habit of eating away at you, and sometimes to preserve your peace of mind and minimise the damage to your health, you need to let go of things and accept at times it is impossible to know the answer to every problem. Instead, you should focus on living life without a huge 'thought cloud' constantly hovering above you, following you everywhere.

Through an honest acceptance of this, you will be able to breathe again and live your life to the maximum as opposed to allowing the unknown to continually throttle your system. There are some things in life that need to be laid to rest; otherwise they will eat away at you until the only thing that will be resting in peace will be... yes, you got it!

Another way to look at this, is to replace the energy you are unnecessarily consuming (akin to the wheels of a car stuck in a mud pit continuously going round in circles), with positive energy that helps create positive thoughts, which opens doors and moves you forward.

Look after your gums.

5

No more excuses!

You may well say, "Easier said than done Jim! You don't have an abusive or intimidating partner, a bullying boss or colleague, an unruly child or nagging parents..." the list goes on. In fact, I have known people who have had to deal with all four of these types of negative relationships, and the only way they overcame them was by taking positive steps to bring about change. They actually did something, rather than complain about it, that was the difference.

Make that change.

Each and every individual has the ability to change the dynamics of any situation and/or relationship. All you need to do is start looking at things from a different perspective, and focus on a solution rather than the problem itself.

Here is a simple example that illustrates the point:

You have an abusive colleague or boss – what can you do?

1. You look for another job.

2. You consider transferring to another department.

3. You complain to a higher authority within the organisation.

4. You speak to the person directly and tell them how you feel.

5. You seek professional legal advice.

6. You write a letter to the head of the organisation.

7. You do nothing at all and let it continue until one of you eventually leaves.

The purpose of the exercise above is to show you that, in the space of five minutes, I have come up with seven alternatives to deal with the problem. None of these may suit you; however, I am sure you could easily come up with another five.

You must do all that you can to resolve your anguish, not continue to bury your head in the sand. You see, there will come a day when it will have to be resolved one way or another, so you may as well start now and deal with it. At the very least, dig down deep and find the courage to try and find a solution. **Andre Gide** articulates this very well; *"Man cannot discover new oceans unless he has the courage to lose sight of the shore."*

I have always believed that any negativity that comes into your life can be dealt with in one of three ways; you can either let it consume you, in which case it defines you; you allow it to destroy you; you learn from it and let it strengthen you.

Three choices – and I am sure you know which one needs to be made, don't you!

*Two important things in life; never compromise on the quality of a good mattress and good shoes, because if you're not in one, you're always in the other.

6

Life is life – fight for it

"Life is an opportunity – benefit from it,
Life is beauty – admire it,
Life is bliss – taste it,
Life is a dream – realise it,
Life is a challenge – meet it,
Life is a duty – complete it,
Life is a game – play it,
Life is a promise – fulfil it,
Life is sorrow – overcome it,
Life is a song – sing it,
Life is a struggle – accept it,
Life is a tragedy – confront it,
Life is an adventure – dare it,
Life is luck – make it,
Life is too precious – do not destroy it,
Life is life – fight for it!"
~ Mother Teresa

No matter how many times you break down, always dig deep and find that piece of you that says, "*No you are not done yet, get back up!*"

Believe in yourself, and the world will believe in you, do not accept you are second best. In your world, you are number one... and don't ever forget it.

Learn to sit properly, keep your posture upright – look after your back.

7

You and your relationships

My eldest brother has developed the habit of complaining about the world continually letting him down. I often ask him "Why do you have such high expectations of people in the first place? Is it them or is it you who is at fault?"

"You are the sum of the relationships you keep."

You must have heard the phrase *"You are the sum of the relationships you keep"*? I firmly believe that the only way you can improve your life is by surrounding yourself with people who can support you to move forward.

I also believe that you hold the master key to each of your relationships, only you, and you alone can dictate how you want to shape those relationships and where you want them to go. The difficulty we have is that we allow others to dictate the terms, and when we do that we are not in control and become vulnerable to their behaviour. What's more, our expectations are continually in danger of never being met, which then creates a blame culture we start to rely on.

Anthony Hopkins effectively conveys this point in simple terms *"Do not expect anything and accept everything."* I do love this quote - in other words, give without expectation.

You see the reality is, you come into this world on your own, and you will also one day leave alone. To make your life a happier one, you form relationships, but no matter how strong they are or will become, you will always be on your own in terms of your journey as the only person you can ever rely on is you. Although your friendships and bonds may be as solid as a rock, eventually over time, due to changes in your environment, in the people that you meet, and in the challenges you face, you will find that you will be the one constant throughout. This is why it is important to live your life as positively as possible and not through someone else.

Only you can allow yourself to be hurt - open the door and make it easier for others to share a good relationship with you and remember it is *your* life and *you* need to live it.

*Go on, give your parents a hug and a kiss – don't be shy – they are your parents after all!

8

It's your journey

We are all on our own journey – don't compare it with others – just try to enjoy yours! Do not judge another's path, as you have no idea of the journey they have had to endure.

We often spend a lot of time talking about others.

We either find ourselves envious of other people's lives or irritated by our own when comparing it with others. Wrong attitude and wrong approach! You will never find peace or happiness when comparing anything to what someone else has. Be happy with who you are and where you are. A good stabiliser to remember is that there will always be people better and worse off than yourself; don't knock down your house just because you have seen a castle.

There is nothing wrong with being inspired to achieve what others have achieved, but this has to be done with a positive attitude, where you are inspired by the other person's achievement, and feel good about yourself in wanting to achieve a higher goal or quality of life. If you use the wrong equation of envy or frustration, you will only dig yourself a deeper hole. Negativity is a sure way of destroying as opposed to nurturing.

"Remember, when people undermine your dreams, predict your doom, or criticise you, they are telling you their own story, not yours." ~ **Cynthia Occelli**

Twelve months from this very day, at least 100 self-made millionaires will appear from nowhere, including sports people, artists and writers, etc., they will be recognised and will have created their own success. They are not there yet, but trust me, they will be. Some are gifted in their chosen field, but others are just bold and focused enough in what they want to achieve.

Whatever age we are, we should look forward to what we can be and what we can create as opposed to saying, *"Look at him, didn't he do well? I wish I could have done that when I had the chance."*

I am a great believer that it is never too late, you just need to get on and do it, as opposed to continually talk about it - a bit like this book, that I have been meaning to write for many years!

The idea is simple; whilst you are still breathing you will always have the opportunity to better yourself and your circumstances, it just requires some self belief, focus and hard work.

* *Do not continually use and breathe in cleaning products and detergents.*

9

A little bit of love
goes a long, long way

*Whatever you do, do it with love. You make a living by what
you earn, you make a life by what you give.*

A good investment.

Some people find these words cheesy and think that this way of
thinking is impractical. Whether or not this axiom is practical, cheesy
or irrelevant, just try it – trust me it can make a big difference to the
party receiving the love.

As hard as someone's exterior may seem, when you embrace that
person with love and attention, you actually start to melt down their
barriers even if just for a short while.

It may not be the norm for you, and you may feel uncomfortable at first, but when you show love with sincerity, you can achieve so much more in relationships and life, and you will receive more in return than you can imagine.

One of those magical moments in my life was a story relayed to me by my partner. During a fête at a school my eldest son used to attend, she bumped into one of the other mothers who told my partner how happy she was to see her and asked about our son's well-being, expressing what a lovely boy he was. Jokingly my partner replied that he had his moments!

To which she remarked how proud she was of him as he had made a major impact on her own son's life, recalling a story some years back when the class went on a camping trip. Five team captains were chosen to pick who would be in their tent. The five chosen were the most popular in their class. My son was asked to go first as he was a team captain, and he immediately picked the two most unpopular boys to share his tent, one of the boys being her son, knowing that they would be the last to be picked. That one act of forethought and kindness gave her son so much confidence that she saw an instant difference in him.

Of course, as parents this story gives us great joy, but what was so beautiful about it is how a little bit of gracious discretion can go a very long way.

*Don't worry, none of us are perfect, we all make mistakes... don't be too hard on yourself, learn to love yourself more.

10

Laugh and be happy

Just for a few minutes, allow your mind to wander back to a day when someone or something made you really happy and you laughed naturally without feeling you had to. What was it that made you smile?

Smile from the heart.

We default to being mature and sensible as we grow older as it is what is expected given our age, and we would look silly laughing all the time, wouldn't we? However, growing older doesn't mean you are not allowed to have fun anymore; presuming you had fun in the first place. It doesn't mean you can't smile more often than being serious, and it doesn't mean you can't express the power of positivity to those around you. As you get older, you should be leading the way by encouraging others to laugh and be happy – I am guessing that some of you are old enough to understand where I am coming from – if anyone should know, you should!

This is especially important for those of us who are so busy trying to earn an income to make ends meet, we too should not forget to laugh – it is healthy for the mind and soul! After reading this statement, some of you may well be saying, *"yes Jim, easier said than done!"* (Kindly re-acquaint yourself with the contents of Chapter 2.)

Remember to try and give your brain a break daily. Your mind does not always need to be defensive, sceptical or practical, let it roam, enjoy and experience life in all its beauty. Let it be. Stop and relax.

The time you spend dallying in the negative zone is a complete waste of time and energy. It does nothing to take you forward, it simply feeds your own issues and insecurities. Yes, that's right, we all have them; they just come in different quantities – big and small. You need to start working on reducing these, it is really not that difficult.

If you don't take steps to make yourself aware of these negative 'monkeys' that keep jumping around in the brain, then after a while this negative thinking penetrates your subconscious, and the mind becomes one that can only operate if there is negativity seeping through. Criticism and complaints become the norm in your everyday life, and this is neither good for your health or outlook.

Stop for a few minutes today and think about an event or person that has made you smile from the heart. Remind yourself exactly what inspired you, and keep hold of that thought for as long as you can. That feeling of happiness and inspiration will influence your day and slowly filter itself into your being. Keep the pilot light on at all times!

Capture your grandparents' history on tape as it will be lost once they have gone.

11

Keep it simple

The best things in life come in the form of simplicity through children and relationships

Keep your relationships simple.

Children simply want your time and for you to be fully engaged with them during those precious moments. Nothing complicated, just recognition and love. Children would much rather have just five minutes of quality time with you, (and by this I mean fully engaged, with no distractions) than five distracted hours (such as watching TV or on your mobile or computer). Simple.

Trust me, the best things in life are found in those special simple moments and acts of endearment.

Complicate relationships and they will become a nightmare. Keep them straightforward and simple; people know where they stand, and expectations are kept in check.

By the way, you probably won't believe this, but guess what? There was once life before mobile phones and emails. We only have ourselves to blame for reducing the quality of our lives and increasing the stress and pressure. People have always made a living, and the commercial world has been going around the block at a certain pace for many years. But recently we have increased that speed, it is like watching the speedometer in your car go up. We are no longer cruising at a steady 70 mph but pressing down on the accelerator and hitting 100 mph, the problem being that we are only in second gear!

Please try and keep it simple and increase not decrease your quality of life. Decrease your pressure on the pedal and find your cruise control switch.

Over the years, I have recounted a very well known story to many so that I can bring this point home.

It relates to a Mexican fisherman from a coastal village, who used to fish each morning between five and six. When he came on to the shore and moored his small boat, he carried with him two, possibly three fish.

A high flying executive, on holiday there, watched him each day from his deckchair, and on the seventh day he asked the fisherman what he did with his day and his fish. The fisherman said that he took his children to school, he would do a few odd jobs here and there, he would cook one fish later on in the afternoon and sit with his family to eat, he would go for a walk with his wife and then later in the evening he would meet his friends and cook the other fish. They would have some wine, play some guitar, and then he would start again the next morning.

The executive told him he was mad, and that he had worked out that if he were out in the sea for an extra three hours, the extra three fish he would catch he could sell, and within two years, he would be able to buy another boat. Within five years, he would have 10 people working for him and own eight boats. Within 10 years, he would have over 100 boats and 250 people working for him and within 20 years, he would have an empire and could list his company on the stock exchange. The fisherman then asked the executive, what then Señor?

The executive replied, *"And then my friend, you retire and enjoy life, take your kids to school, eat with the family, go take walks with your wife, spend time, have some wine and play some guitar with your friends in the evenings."* The fisherman answered, *"But Señor that is exactly what I am doing now, why do I need to wait for 20 years to do it...!"*

He certainly left someone speechless.

Stretch for five minutes *every morning.*

12

Health is true wealth

When we see people who train, look fit and eat healthy, we often say, "It would be great to be like that, but it's way too much hassle."

Keep healthy.

For many, the motivation for fad diets and crazy workouts is due to the fact that they want to look and feel good.

In my opinion, the real reason to get in shape is to stay healthy - looking good in the summer is just an added bonus. Keeping your heart protected and healthy for the years ahead is as important for you as it is to those around you.

Avoid over-reliance on daily super foods and intense prolonged physical exercise, as the body only needs a certain amount of healthy food and exercise to keep in shape and remain healthy. You get into trouble when you either stop the super foods or the intense exercise, as the body reacts in a certain way when it doesn't get what it has become accustomed to, and for some it could mean piling on the pounds.

It really is amazing what you can do with the body if you don't raise its expectations. I am no doctor, nutritionist or health consultant, I am just telling you from the little bit I know about my body, how it works and with a touch of common sense.

If you gradually introduce good healthy foods and exercise as part of your life, as opposed to imposing it as a heavy daily obligation, (only to give up the healthy regime a few weeks later) can really work in your favour in the long term – have you heard the story of the tortoise and the hare? Well, I am guessing you know who won that particular race! This really can work well in the long term.

Always remember the best nutritional food in life is positive thought, everything else is just supplementary.

Try and make time for your partner, parents, children and siblings more often.

13

Let them talk

It's none of your business what others think of you!

Do not live your life by listening to what others say about you.

One of my favourite stories that really brings this point to life, relates to a donkey, a father and his son. One day they were walking through their neighbouring village with the boy riding on the donkey. As they were passing through, they overheard a villager comment on how disrespectful the son was, as his father was walking while the son was sitting on the donkey. The son then got off and switched with his father and, as they passed the next village, they overheard the villagers gossiping about how selfish the father was for riding the donkey while his young boy was walking. The father asked the boy to get on the donkey, and they both rode the donkey into the next village. The villagers remarked how cruel the father and son were as they were both sitting on the poor donkey. Having heard this, the father and son got off the donkey and, as they passed through the next village, they overheard a villager say that the boy and the father were both fools as no one was sitting on the donkey – at which point both the son and father picked up the donkey. The donkey, who was obviously unhappy about the situation, jumped and kicked, landed in a river and drowned. The father and son sat by the river bank and looked at each other and said, *"How stupid we are, having listened to all those villagers, we now have no donkey!"*

We allow ourselves to be easily influenced by third–party comments, but who is the best person to tell you what you are all about? Correct – you!

No one knows you better than yourself. You have first-hand knowledge, and hopefully an honest assessment of your strengths and weaknesses. Third parties come into their understanding of us by way of second hand knowledge, which is often inaccurate. They could also have a hidden agenda. You know who you are, so listen to yourself and not to what other people think of you. You are the expert in the ring, and they are mere spectators.

If, however, you doubt your own opinion in any way, then find someone who truly loves you and ask them for their honest, non–judgemental opinion, just in case you have a blind spot concerning your own abilities..

As much as this may apply to people talking about you, it equally applies to you talking about other people (we all do it!). So next time you find yourself about to do this, first ask yourself three questions;

1. Is what I'm about to say about that person positive or negative?

2. Am I sure that what I'm about to say about that person 100% correct?

3. Is what I'm about to say about that person benefitting me in any way?

In answering these questions, some of us may find that what we say is not always positive, it's never 100% accurate, and the only benefit is a momentary feeling of smugness.

There is nothing wrong with a gossip every now and then, however, if you dish it out, then be prepared... I think you get the picture!

Focus on living, rather than worrying about what others think of you and what you might think of them.

We pack three times
more than we need when
travelling. It's a waste of
fuel, energy and bad for
the back.

*

14

Do you know your weaknesses?

*Every one of us has weaknesses, but many of us
don't like to admit to them, not even to ourselves –
that is the worrying bit!*

What are yours?

OK, I can understand you do not want to tell me or the person next to you, but come on, you can at least be honest with yourself in the privacy of a quiet room – I can promise you, no one is listening. It is OK to just say to yourself, *"Do you know what? I'm actually quite self-centred... at times, I do drink too much ... sometimes I do get angry way too quickly..."* and so on.

You probably have about one or two major weaknesses, and a few niggly ones (don't worry about the rest). You don't need to delve into the past and think about why you have them unless they are heavily influencing your relationships. You just need to accept that you do have them, and that they don't enhance your life but have become a hindrance and a liability. You need to work out a game plan to deal with them the next time they rear their ugly heads. If they come around regularly and have a negative impact on your environment, then sort it out sooner rather than later. Once you apply your mind, and accept that you have these weaknesses, only then can you work on diminishing them. After doing so, you start to lighten the burden you carry around, helping your communication and relationships with others.

Life's challenges come in different shapes and sizes, and are not there to paralyse you, but to help you learn and discover who you are.

I would suggest that you take some time out today. Go to a private room, look at yourself in the mirror (make sure no one is around), and ask yourself out loud – what are your two biggest weaknesses? Don't worry, no one is listening. You will get there eventually, and when you do, you will need to start making positive and practical steps to make these demons a thing of the past. The secret to making this work effectively is for you to be *completely honest* with yourself.

You may, however, be one of those people who feels that you don't need to change your weaknesses as they can sometimes work to your benefit (anger, for example) and, therefore, are worth keeping, but I don't agree. If you think that it is a weakness, then why carry it around? You are probably confusing it with an occupational asset – it is not – trust me!

Do not ignore, defend or protect your deficiencies. Confront them with a view to reducing them!

Taking lemon and probiotics daily is great for the digestive system.

15

Where are the crutches?

Your body and mind are stronger than you think.

You have the tools to help yourself!

The reality is that we find ourselves looking for support from 'crutches' long before we need them. I am no doctor, but I do know that on some occasions when the chips are down, and the body and mind are weak, *you* have to conjure up the strength to deal with things yourself, rather than turning the situation into an international crisis by rounding up help and support from all and sundry. You see, when the problem gets resolved, or subsides, you often kick yourself for letting the whole world know about it when actually you had all the tools within to resolve the situation, you just needed to listen and believe.

Sharing a problem with someone else lightens the burden, there is no doubt, but relying on someone to support you by way of 'crutches' weakens your resolve to fend for yourself. It is a bit like building up your own immune system as opposed to rushing off to take antibiotics the minute you can't shake off a cough. There are many problems you can deal with by using *your* mental strength and personal resolve to find a way forward.

Eventually, you will come up with the right answer. Doing this will allow you to become your very own self-help guru with the ability to remedy any difficulties that come your way. It gives you self-worth and a sense of achievement; it is a great feeling!

A very brave and amazing example of this relates to a dear friend of mine, Pal, who helped me rebuild a badly damaged rotator cuff tear in my right shoulder through his brilliant personal training sessions.

Late one evening, a few years ago, whilst he was returning home from work on his bicycle, a crazed man, who was twice his size, carrying an eight-inch knife, attacked him a few feet away from his front door. The knife penetrated his skull, severing his optic nerve as well as going through the bone in his left arm. After struggling with the psychotic man, he managed to get free and run away.

As he broke loose there were two things going through his mind; firstly, that he should try to get the man away from his front door since he was worried that his wife, (hearing the commotion), may open the door and also fall victim; secondly, he knew he had to run and fall where someone would find and help him; or else he could be lying there, in the dark street and most certainly die from blood loss as his main arteries had been severed.

Now, I was meant to see him the next day, so when I didn't hear from him I eventually located him at the Royal Free Hospital, in a harrowing state. At first it was hard to take in. I tried to hide my shock and spoke to him as if all was well, but inside I knew it was so far from the truth.

His account of the incident made my hair stand on end, and as I stood there speechless, he declared, *"Don't worry about me, Jim, I'm very happy"*. When I asked him why, he replied, *"For two reasons. One being I can still see out of my right eye and two, I'm alive!"* Within six weeks, Pal was back in the gym doing what he does best, training people to get physically and mentally fit!

Incredible! An inspiration if ever there was one.

Remember, dig deep and the find the strength and confidence you need as there is always a way through. Remember that on the other side of fear, lies freedom. Sometimes, you will need to work out for yourself when you actually need 'crutches', but try not to go in too early as this could be a hindrance instead of a help. You just need to make sure that when you eventually *do* need support, you select someone that will give you the right advice and encouragement. Only you can work out who and what that is.

If you believe in yourself, others will do so too.

P.S. When I asked Pal if it was okay to use his story as an example in this chapter, he agreed. As I was leaving he made this passing comment *"Oh, by the way Jim, it wasn't six weeks to get back into work, it was only three!"*

Good one – thanks Pal!

Get an alarm clock that * wakes you up with soothing gentle music not one that is annoying – it ensures a good start to the day.

16

Take advantage of
your strengths

*We all have strengths, some of which we are aware of and
others of which we are not. Be resourceful with your strengths.*

You need to look at your strengths as assets.

Using your strengths is the real route to achieving your true potential.
In the commercial world, businessmen and entrepreneurs are skillful
at using their strengths to extract the most out of them. This is called
'leveraging your assets'. Why shouldn't we do the same with our
strengths? You see, our strengths actually define us.

The difficulty we have is that sometimes we don't always want to talk
about them, for fear that this will come across as boastful and/or
conceited.

The first step in recognising your strengths is to write down areas in which you feel you excel in terms of your personality and/or skills. Then, think about how you can best use these to help develop yourself at work, in your relationships and in achieving your goals. The secret is to keep writing, even if what you are writing makes no sense, even if you have been through a whole book with notes but still cannot find the answer – don't worry, it will come. Circle the points and highlight the key words and you will get closer to identifying your strengths.

If after trying this, you still can't get there, then pick up the phone and speak to a close family member or a loyal friend and arrange to meet. Talk about the goals you have set yourself and then discuss the strengths you have identified, those that you need to cultivate and establish a game plan for how you expect to accomplish them. This friend should be able to objectively identify your strengths, even ones that you can't see. In this way, you will better understand and manage personal relationships and perfect your outlook.

John Wooden conveys this point very eloquently when he articulates; *"Do not let what you cannot do interfere with what you can do."*

* *Take control, don't lose it – count to 20 backwards before lashing out as your tongue can be very destructive!*

17

Your happiness rests with you

"Happiness is a bit like a butterfly..." and is determined by your attitude, not your accomplishments.

Happiness really does rest with you.

I remember when my youngest son turned one year old, and we decided to hold a party to celebrate; with a crowd of almost 500 people, my youngest daughter, at the tender age of seven, went up on stage, took hold of the microphone and boldly declared that she would like to give her brother a gift. Bizarrely, but magically, she then proceeded to quote Nathaniel Hawthorne:

"Happiness is a bit like a butterfly; if you try to catch one, it's always just beyond your grasp, but if you sit down quietly it will come and alight upon you."

To this day we can only assume that she had picked this up from one of my wife's numerous quotation books! I absolutely loved it - pure magic!

I appreciate I have laboured on this point already in the book, but because of its importance I believe I need to re-emphasise the principle behind it.

We have all, at one point or another, suffered from problems in the past or are suffering from them at present. However, the way we approach and confront these has a profound impact on our happiness. You see, happiness is not found in the absence of problems but in how you tackle and resolve them. Problems are an inevitable part of life, but if you want to dwell on them and make them an integral part of your everyday life, then that is your choice. Alternatively you can put them into perspective and deal with them practically and constructively one at a time.

There are some problems in life that no matter what you do you will never be able to resolve. There is no point worrying about these, as they will waste your time and energy. However, problems that you *can* do something about should be confronted as soon as possible as they require a frank and honest assessment, so that you can solve them with minimum damage to yourself and others. When you have figured this out, you then need to find the courage to tackle them head on!

An interesting take on creating your own happiness comes from a story I heard many years ago, about two patients in a hospital ward with beds next to each other, one was next to the window, the other not. Each day the patient next to the window would tell his neighbour of all the lovely things he could see outside. His neighbour had a broken back and was bed-ridden, so he relied on all that he heard from the other. Each day the man's description of the outside world, the green lawns, the birds singing and the children playing, would lift and inspire the other man.

Sadly, one afternoon the man by the window passed away. So his neighbour with the broken back asked the nurse to tell him about what was going on outside the window. The nurse replied by saying there was nothing going on outside as there was only an ugly big brick wall in front of the window. How strange, thought the man and he asked the nurse why his friend would want to mislead him for so many months, telling him these wonderful stories about life outside. The nurse replied that the man who had passed away was, in fact, blind and that he had obviously told those stories to his friend to keep him inspired and keep him holding on to the will to live by describing the beauty of the outside world, as opposed to burdening him with sorrow.

This man despite his disability chose to inspire himself and did not let his disability weigh him down and become a burden. He chose to see what he wanted to see in order to lift his world and lift the world of those around him.

My philosophy is pretty straightforward; your happiness believe it or not, rests in your hands and not simply in the circumstances or the cards you have been dealt. There are close to seven billion people on this planet. Each of us has been dealt a unique set of cards which include your country of origin, your race, your culture, your parents and your circumstances. We have to accept that we are all individuals and that none of these cards are perfect. We need to acknowledge that we are where we are and once we have accepted our hand, only then can we move on and decide how that hand can be played. This will make all the difference between where you are today and where you could be tomorrow.

Only you can change your circumstances, by taking some form of positive action to resolve your problems and create opportunities to make your life that little bit better and that little bit happier each day – no more excuses and no more playing the victim.

Never allow your mind and body to retire, keep the engine running at all times.

18

At times do you feel all alone?

Mother Teresa once said, "Being unwanted, unloved, uncared for or forgotten, is a much greater hunger and a much greater poverty than the person who has nothing to eat."

The greatest gift you can give is sharing your time.

Mother Teresa is the only individual I have felt it necessary to reference a number of times in this book. This woman really got it, and with simplicity and intelligence she tried to convey her message and principles to the world.

The greatest gift you can give is to share your time and love with people who feel alone – it would mean more to them than giving them a bag of gold. Trust me, they will really appreciate and respect the value of your time and company.

We are so busy with our own lives that we don't see the real loneliness in others, even when they are right under our nose. People often suffer in silence, or when they do cry out for help, we fail to acknowledge them. We programme our minds to ignore the person and their problems, because we make it out to be an issue that it's too difficult and too complicated for us to help them with, either that, or we are just too busy with our own lives to spend the time worrying about someone else. We could all do with a wake-up call in this department and be more aware of the people around us.

By learning to be more receptive to others, you will ensure that the world will become more connected – and more importantly it is an amazing gift to leave behind for our next generation.

*If you can't handle your drink, then give it up! The two of you were not meant to be together, and we all know that unhappy partnerships are destructive!

19

Look forward to one thing each day

A simple way of getting some meaning into your life is to devote yourself to creating something that gives you purpose and meaning each day.

Do not waste a single day of your life.

Some people walk around as if they have a meaningless life. They seem to be half asleep, even when they are busy doing things that would be considered important. This is because many people are chasing either the wrong goals, or none at all.

Think of life being akin to a meter in a taxi, where you have been given an allowance of a full one mile ride each day. My philosophy is to use up that one mile journey, not more, not less. Do not save the miles for tomorrow or use up the credit of more than one mile in a day. That way you will enjoy as much as you can each day of your life, or at least you will do your very best to do so.

When you wake up in the morning, decide on what it is you are going to look forward to that day. It could be cooking a special yet simple meal in the evening, seeing an old friend, watching a movie, writing poetry, painting or even making time to sing with the kids – whatever it may be, make it exciting and special for you. If you do this, you will feel a lot more positive and content about your day.

By making the most of each day, you will ensure that you make the most of your life. It is interesting how **Francis Bacon** simplifies this in his quote: *"Hope is a good breakfast but a bad supper."* It is always good to start the day with hope and anticipation for the exciting moments to come in the day, but if you are still waiting by supper time with only hope then it is useless.

Results require action, it is the one difference between staying put and creating change.

Cut out the white bread and white sugar.

20

The London cab driver

It is all about perspective!

"So how has your day been so far?"

Whenever I sit in the back of a London black cab, I always ask the driver, "So, how has your day been so far?" Of course, the replies I get are varied. Some are miserable, short and spiky as they have been stuck in traffic all day, whilst others are chirpy, positive and talkative about the very fact that they at least have a job (traffic for them not being an issue). I tell the pessimistic ones that driving a cab and being stuck in traffic is part and parcel of the job they do, and they are much better off factoring this in before starting their day.

In other words, one driver can take the approach and attitude that there will be a fair amount of traffic on the roads that day, but if they get a clear stretch then that is a bonus, while another may expect a traffic–free run so the minute they hit traffic they get upset and frustrated.

The first approach keeps you calm and positive as you have already factored the difficulties into your expectations of the day. Alternatively, the second choice, which is based upon unrealistic expectations, places you in a position to be let down time and time again, which ultimately fosters negativity. It all comes down to the choices and expectations you make first thing in the morning. This analogy could equally be applied to your relationships and the building up of expectations that may be unrealistic.

Alexander Pope sums this up pretty well; *"Blessed is he who expects nothing, for he shall never be disappointed."*

Remember no relationship is perfect. Going back to the 70% rule, as long as the bulk of the relationship is positive, a few hiccups along the way won't rock the boat. Do not expect a perfect ride otherwise you are setting yourself up for disappointment.

In addition to keeping expectations in check, it is equally important to constantly keep life in perspective, as I mentioned at the beginning.

When we hear of a tragedy , we say to ourselves , that story really puts life into perspective – but how long does this feeling last? When we make New Years resolutions, we say *"this time I am going to stick to it!"* – really? How long does it last? When you read the quirky one liner in this book at Chapter 6, about keeping your posture straight, I'm guessing you immediately sat up and now you have reverted to sitting in the same crouched position as before. How long did that last?

The point here is that keeping life in perspective must be part of our everyday thinking, rather than just a temporary thought.

Try and keep one central location in the house for the internet, entertainment, TV, music, etc. Better your children are interacting with you than away in their individual rooms.

21

Only one set of shoulders – easy on the weight

We only have one set of shoulders, and there is only so much weight we can carry on them.

It's not about solving all the world's problems!

You are not superman or superwoman, and whilst you may try to carry all this weight, remember you do not have to solve all the world's problems on your own.

Of course, it is always a good thing to try and help others, but only as long as the output improves the input. You do not want to add to a problem or end up having to off-load it if it becomes too much. Take on what you can, but remember it is not about solving the world's problems and forgetting to live, it is about living whilst resolving the problems you can comfortably manage without causing suffering to yourself and those around you.

Drink plenty of water to ***** *keep the body and mind hydrated at all times.*

22

Congratulations!
You have won the lottery

I believe you have won the lottery each day,
you just don't know it!

Congratulations!

There are two neighbours who are both feeling down. One is upset because he has had an accident in his new car, the other is upset because he has just lost his job and has a family of five to feed. Both feel devastated and need time to get over it. In fact, both have spent the weekend at home depressed and have taken their frustration out on those around them.

If you had a choice, you know which neighbour's shoes you would rather be in. I certainly do. The chap whose car door is slightly damaged is rightly upset, but when he learns of his neighbour's fate it puts his circumstances into perspective. The neighbour wasted a weekend of valuable time worrying when he could have spent quality time with his family. His problem is minute in comparison to his neighbour's.

It is like the classic story of the man who complains about having to walk many miles in broken shoes, and at the end of the journey he meets a man with no feet. By that time, it is too late as he has already wasted the journey complaining and being upset with everyone along the way, but when he sees the man with no feet, suddenly all is put into perspective. On the next occasion, he will look at things differently, even with broken shoes.

If you can see, hear, feel, taste, walk and talk, as far as I am concerned, you are already way ahead of the game, but sometimes we do not appreciate these special gifts. It is when you don't have one of them, or when it has been taken from you, that you actually realise how lucky you were.

If you have good health, then don't take it for granted, please try and look after it, as it is akin to winning the lottery each day – trust me on that!

* *No matter how important you think you are, just remember, we are all dispensable!*

23

Give with *your* hands

*The gift of giving with your own hands cannot
be measured.*

Give with your own hands.

The power and beauty of giving something to someone that improves
the quality of their life, even in the slightest way is immense. You have
to experience it to truly understand it. When you give with your own
hands it makes the experience that much more fulfilling. Some people
do give by credit or debit card, but sometimes due to time or other
responsibilities cannot always be there to give themselves. But if they
did take time out of their busy diaries once in a while, to physically
give themselves to the needy and vulnerable, then it really would make
all that they are doing worthwhile.

Some people don't share or disclose their giving nature with others and prefer to keep it quiet and confidential as they are afraid that this will come across as boastful, or just simply want to keep their business to themselves. However in my view, sharing the beauty of donating with others in order to inspire them, is much more real, significant and special.

I have been very fortunate to see this within my own children from an early age. One of my beautiful moments was a story told by my son's schoolteacher, again years after he had left school. At the age of nine, for weeks my son came home from school with porridge stains all over his washed and ironed school sweater. My partner's patience was wearing thin, and she warned my son that if his sweater was dirty again the next day he would be punished. Sure enough, those stains reappeared, and he was duly reprimanded. Then one afternoon, years later, my partner got talking to our son's old teacher, who was full of praise for my son's commitment to the Downs Syndrome children who were housed across the road from the school. Every afternoon he would go and feed them their lunch – hence the porridge stains. He never told us, even to this day.

In Sanskrit, giving is called "Seva" and without doubt, if there was one of life's gifts I would wish for above all else, it would be the gift of giving without seeking anything in return, other than the knowledge that you have contributed towards the well being of another. It is certainly the most complete and satisfying of them all.

I have also experienced giving through the work of certain organisations that are passionately involved with the protection of children, and three organisations (based in the UK, India and Guatemala) have been a real inspiration to me over the years as to what can be achieved through hard work, sincerity and dedication to the cause.

*	*Try and regulate your body to clear the bowels each morning.*

24

Life's special moments

Capture those special moments with those special people in an imaginary glass bottle – they're worth their weight in gold.

Glass bottle moments.

There are moments in your life that should be captured and preserved in a glass bottle, so you can relive them at any time. Replaying these moments takes you back in time and allows you to reminisce on those special memories, and releases endorphins into your bloodstream.

Often, children say funny things that are so completely left field that it catches you unaware, and you cannot help but smile like a Cheshire cat, even when they are being naughty. Maybe you have been with friends or a partner, and someone says something so unexpected, it has you in complete stitches. Even though you can't always record these moments, there is no reason why you can't just capture them in your mind and place them in an imaginary glass bottle.

These are golden moments that make life worth living. Constantly try to put yourself in an environment which induces these moments to come around more often. At an appropriate time, reflect on them and thoroughly enjoy them, then put them into a bottle for life to enjoy later. Trust me, this bottle that contains your special moments will be one of your most treasured possessions later in life.

If the bottle concept seems a little intangible to you (or if you are forgetful), you could try carrying a small notebook with you at all times. For instance, your children will say many things that will open up your heart and light up your face as they are growing up – jot these down. Trust me, many years later you or your children will read over them and enjoy them with the same intensity as you originally did. It is moments like these that constitute the real value in our lives.

Here is one of my glass bottle moments that I cherish.

One day, when my eldest son was about three, his mother told him that if he was a good boy she would give him a treat (as you do). Well he had behaved himself all day and approached his mother for his reward. She frantically searched the cupboards for something to give him. The only thing she found was chocolate finger biscuits which were quite small *"oh it's a chocolate finger – wow!"* She could see the disappointment in his eyes and felt bad as she didn't have anything more to give him. He too didn't want to come across greedy, but his reply was *"mummy, I didn't want a finger... I wanted the whole hand!"*

Priceless!

Try not to use soap on your face too often and always wash with cold/luke warm water.

25

Just set some goals, any will do, but just do it please.

Don't just follow your dreams – chase them!

Set yourself some goals.

A request from me is to please set yourself some goals this year, no matter how ambitious or trivial they maybe. Don't wait for the beginning of the year by way of a New Year's resolution, do it now, whatever the day, even whilst reading this chapter.

Don't worry about how crazy they may sound, or how simple and boring they may be. Everyone has some ambition inside them, something they have wanted to do and someone they aspire to be. If that ambition is as dead as a dodo, then get yourself down to the accident and emergency department and get it revived – NOW!

Start writing down your goals/dreams. Make time for this, all you need is a quiet 30 minutes to contemplate what they are.

You need a place of quiet contemplation to bring these thoughts to the fore.

This exercise helps tremendously as it stops you drifting from one year to another without having any ambition or drive. It is in your hands whether you want to step onto the path of self achievement and success or just sit there and continue to blame your job, your partner, your kids, your life, your circumstances, your health, etc. Success means different things to different people. Whatever you aspire to in life, take that first step today, and you will thank yourself in years to come that you did.

Identify what it is you want to do and then start to talk about it with others – don't be shy, just do it – you will be surprised how many people want to hear it and say *"You know what, that's what I have always wanted to do too."*

When you realise that other individuals echo your dreams and goals, you will feel inspired and more confident to pursue them. Despite doing things for those around us, we must fulfil our own aspirations along the way, don't let yourself down. If you are still reading, that is a good sign as it means that the heart and mind are still ticking and therefore you still have time to set some goals.

Be an inspiration to others.

Use almond or mustard oil and give yourself a body massage twice a month.

26

The virtues of garlic, ginger, chilli, lemon & turmeric

Yes, I am of Indian origin, and no I don't have shares in the agriculture industry relating to any of these foods!

Introduce these items into your daily diet.

The benefits of these are unbelievable. The best thing about these foods is that when they are all mixed together in one pot, the combination tastes pretty amazing. You will have food that is not only very good for your health but tastes pretty good too – what more can you ask for?

Start to give some thought towards what you consume each day, as it really does have a major impact on how you feel, how you think, and your everyday interactions with others. Your body and food cannot live without each other , they are both a significant part of your being, so please give them the respect they jointly deserve.

*

Try to use less of the WiFi when you're out – try talking to each other, like the good old days!

27

Same old... day in, day out

Stuck in a rut? Tired of the same journey into work?
Eating the same food? Following the same routine every day?

Oh dear me!

Many of us go through good days and bad days. We become frustrated with the tedious routine we have to follow to make ends meet. The monotony of everyday life, in the workforce or at home, can bring with it highs and lows which at times can lead to loneliness and depression.

You may feel trapped or bored, or feel like you are wasting each year. The only thing you have to look forward to is your annual holiday or time off. What you don't realise, however, is that you can actually use the windows of time between your daily activities much more effectively. You will be an hour, a day, a week, a month and a year older when you let time go by without making the most it. Remember, there is no rewind button and it can all be over in a flash.

So, again you say, *"Easier said than done, Jim, but there simply are not enough hours in the day to make the most of my time."*

I read a quote a few years ago, which said, *"I freed a thousand slaves and could have freed thousands more, if only they knew that they were slaves."* **~ Harriet Tubman.**

The point here is you go out into the field, collect the corn in a sack and then carry the heavy load on your back up the hill, every day, without giving real thought as to why - other than to earn money to provide security for you and your family. Then one fine day your body and or mind gives up, and you have a revelation. *"What the heck was that all about, there was so much more I could have done than just carry that sack up and down that hill for the last 40 years!"*

Don't go through life as a means to an end! Stop and smell the flowers along the way. Make the changes needed to enjoy every moment.

What you have to do is try and inspire yourself with something new, whether it is aiming for a promotion at work, educating yourself on a new topic, trying out a new or old sport you enjoyed, learning a language or simply starting to read again. Whatever it is, no matter how bizarre or left of field, renew that vigour, you won't regret it!

Always remember, inspiration comes slowly and quietly, use the solitude to reflect and get the best from it.

So in terms of putting this into practise, a method that I find helpful is to write down some positive reinforcements that are simple to follow.

The headings below are a good start.

JOB – PROMOTION

FINANCES – SAVINGS

RELATIONSHIP – IMPROVEMENT

HOBBIES – RESTART

CHARITY – GET INVOLVED

HEALTH – REJUVENATE

FOOD – CREATE

FRIENDS AND FAMILY – RECONNECT

I have made an attempt at taking you through how best to tackle each heading on the following pages.

THERE IS NOTHING WRONG IN ASPIRING TO ACHIEVE A GREATER ROLE IN YOUR WORK.

Job – Promotion

Get on the internet and find out what opportunities are available to ascend the occupational ladder. You may want to explore similar positions, or find out about new ideas or processes in your existing position, that will bring about change and excitement to the business you are in. This will challenge your mind and demonstrate that you are not trapped in just one place and to one process – there are other opportunities out there that can release the shackles and give you the chance to spread your wings. The world really is a big place. You do need to check it out!

It is always a good idea to make a list of all your key contacts that can help. Go through your mobile phone, and make a list of 10 important people you can meet face to face, who can help give you constructive ideas and/or introduce you to others, who are better placed to help you further your career.

Take time to make the right choice, but know in your mind that there are thousands of occupations and even more opportunities around the globe. Circumstances aside, this essentially means that you have the agency and liberty to pursue whatever you desire.

As they say, aim for the stars and should you not get there, at least you have a good chance of landing on the moon. (Or is that the other way round?!)

There is no need to cry over spilt milk – it's already spilt.

KEEP THE BOOKS BALANCED BUT DON'T FORGET TO LIVE.

Finances – Savings

You will be surprised how easily you can reduce your expenses and start saving, once you have been brave enough to honestly look at your monthly expenditure in detail (and yes, this *includes* looking at your credit card statements!). Remember, although using credit may provide short-term satisfaction, it is exactly that - a quick fix. Don't forget, there is no such thing as free money... you always have to pay it back! By reducing your spending and translating this surplus into your savings, you will automatically feel good, and moreover this feeling won't be short-lived! On the contrary, saving money provides you with a long-term high and will bring many benefits.

By not proactively dealing with your spending and saving habits, you could be leaking money or incurring high interest charges. If you still can't find the time or energy to deal with it, you need to at least realise that you are carrying unnecessary weight around with you, (by having this debt) which is slowing you down. Another way of helping to tackle this issue is to view it from another angle. Any savings you make *could* be given to someone whose life you could change for the better.

I have a little bit of money in a savings account in India, not much but enough to provide me with food and drink when I visit. The account doesn't attract a higher rate of interest as I need to have access to it whenever I am there. A few years ago, a close friend of mine who works in an orphanage, requested my assistance to help a blind child who was expected to leave and make a living for himself as he had come of age. The interest alone from the small deposit was enough to give him a basic living and a chance in life to educate himself without wondering where his next meal was coming from. I still speak to this child regularly and feel comfortable that the money is going direct to the source and is having an immediate effect on the quality of his life.

Make your money work for you, or even better for someone else that needs it!

If you don't step forward, you will always find yourself in the same place.

RELATIONSHIPS - DON'T GET SUCKED INTO THE 'IT'S ALL OVER' CULTURE.

Relationships - Improvement

There are always ways to improve your relationships if you feel they are not working. **Einstein** once defined insanity as *"Doing the same thing over and over again and expecting different results."* For me, there is no greater truth in this when dealing with relationships. Most of them get stuck in a rut with the same monotonous conversations and daily rituals. Change it, shake it up and make it different and you will induce a change in your relationships for the better.

Don't let the change be a one-off thing, keep re-evaluating as you don't want your partner to enquire *"have you been reading 'those' books again?"* Your change has to be genuine, from within and sustainable, otherwise it won't last.

I am not disregarding the fact that there are certain relationships that were never meant to be in the first place, these are simply mismatched. They seriously need to be assessed, as continuing with them may only cause greater suffering. But before doing so, you need to ask yourself, despite your partners shortcomings, are these issues so serious that they are not capable of being fixed?

Don't just simply head off in the direction of 'it's all over'. Give it a long and serious think, speak to those that you trust (in fact, speak to someone who is respected for their honesty, objectivity and impartiality) and after that, decide what is required.

When I see a break-up in a relationship, it makes me question if this will benefit either party. The grass is rarely greener on the other side. You can keep going for many years changing your partner because the connection is not there, and you can keep blaming your partners for the way they are, but actually you may want to take a close look at yourself to see where the real problem lies.

It is a bit like this, people always say there are two sides to every story. Incorrect. There are three. One is theirs, one is yours, and the other... is the truth.

Play hide and seek with your kids and if you are brave enough... with your partner.

WHEN I WAS YOUNGER, I USED TO LOVE PLAYING...

Hobbies – Restart

You must have had some hobbies when you were younger, or at least wanted to do something but never got the chance. Well now is a good time to start. It doesn't have to be expensive or time-consuming, but by factoring it in to your day, you will have something to look forward to and keep your mind active. I can almost hear you say *"I don't have the time, I have mouths to feed."* Well, make the time, it is good for the body and soul.

It really is worth giving it a try. You will, I hope, enjoy rekindling your love for what you enjoyed doing when you were younger.

This may sound somewhat strange, but even at my age, I would love to join a dance group and perform on stage. I love dancing to modern music and I know I would really enjoy it, but whether a younger group of dancers would want me in their group is another story altogether, but you know what, I am going to give it a go anyway as it makes me happy. You should give it some thought too!

Focus on what binds you, not what separates you.

HANDS THAT HELP.

Charities – Get involved

You will be surprised how a tiny bit of involvement in a worthwhile cause can have a major influence on your working day. It will bring you into a zone that will make you appreciate what you may often take for granted. More importantly, you and your contribution as small as it may be, *will* make a positive difference to the lives of those who are less fortunate than you.

When you help others less fortunate, it can teach you a sense of perspective right then and there, without you having to go through something traumatic yourself. This then will let you really appreciate what you have without the 'compare and despair' feeling you can get when you feel you don't have enough.

Get onto the internet and find out about the local charities in your area – it is really easy to get involved, and you will feel that your day has not been wasted – it will give you a sense of purpose. The size of your contribution is irrelevant, what matters is the fact that you have given something, and your direct contribution will make a difference to another person's life. You will never know unless you actually try and make an effort to see if you can help. I do believe that each of us has an obligation and responsibility in life.

Try to cut the carbs out of your diet after 7pm each day.

YES, THAT'S RIGHT, EVEN YOUR BODY CAN FEEL UNLOVED AND UNCARED FOR – DO NOT NEGLECT IT.

Health

You don't need to run the marathon or the three peaks triathlon to keep fit, just some simple exercises at home, at work or in your local park will do. If you keep your body active, you will start to see and feel the difference after a few weeks. Remember, take it easy, go at your own pace, be comfortable and build your programme up slowly around your body. Equally important, is to ensure that your daily diet parallels your healthy lifestyle; otherwise it will just be a   waste of time.

Also, remember to go easy on the artificial products you use on your body. Don't overdo it; the packaging may look great, the advertising sexy and the scent beautiful, but most products should be used sparingly. You need to allow your body to produce the oils it makes naturally, to stop your skin from drying out. If you don't limit your usage, you will appear to age much faster. Swap your chemical products for natural ones wherever possible, as these will assist, in my opinion (I'm no expert, just using a tiny bit of common sense), in slowing down the ageing process.

If you are in a hard water area, install a water softener – the difference is amazing.

WHITE FOODS – NOT SO GOOD.

BROWN FOODS – VERY GOOD.

Food – Create

Give some thought to what you eat every day, and what time you eat it. In fact, for a few days write down everything you consume – kind of like a stock-take of your body – you will be surprised how much bad stuff goes in compared to the healthy stuff!

Try if you can to reduce the bad and increase the good, and try and eat at the right time. I know I am stating the obvious, but it is alarming how many people keep eating unhealthy foods, particularly in between meals when they know it is not good. Don't be one of them as this is not a good long term investment.

Always remember, it has to be dark for the stars to appear, and if you have faith, they will.

THEY ARE WORTH IT.

Friends and Family – Reconnect

It always brings a smile to my face when when an old friend or a member of my family calls out of the blue, just to say hello or to see how I'm doing. It is human nature to be sceptical when this happens and think *"This is very strange, what's going on here, why are they calling me? What does he or she want?"* Yes, some people may have some ulterior motives, but not all do. It is nice to connect with people you haven't spoken to for a long time, and it is remarkable how uplifting this can be for your state of mind. Always make sure you stay in touch, no matter how busy your day – it is so important for your wellbeing.

If you have not spoken to or seen a family friend for years, don't worry, the true test of a genuine friendship is to reconnect from where you left off. Go on, give someone you haven't spoken to in a long time a call, and with whom you have shared a good friendship. In fact, call them before this day is over, you won't regret it.

Making one person smile can change the world – maybe not the whole world, but their world!

28

Remember to lead by example

*We sometimes forget our roles or positions in life.
We tend to go through it forgetting that others may
be relying on us and looking towards us for guidance.*

Think before you act.

In my case, it is my children who are looking to my partner and I, as to how to act at home, outside with others, in social groups and within our wider community. The way we behave will have a significant bearing on the way *they* behave as they grow up – it is inevitable. Therefore, it is important that you think before you act, as the implications of your actions are much more significant than you realise.

There is a Japanese story I heard many years ago, about a wooden bowl which brings this point home perfectly.

A father, his infant son, his wife and his own elderly father sat around the table every evening for dinner. After a few years, the elderly father had problems eating without making a mess, and often dropped his ceramic bowl on the ground. The family decided to move the father off the dinner table and onto the floor in the corner of the room. They placed a plastic cover on the ground, a food bib around his neck and served his meal in a wooden bowl so that it wouldn't break if he dropped it.

This went on for some time, and the elderly father would often shed a silent tear as he was fully aware of what was happening to him. One weekend morning when the father awoke, he saw his four-year-old son in the living room joining pieces of wood together. The father asked what he was making, and the boy replied, *"Daddy, I am making you a wooden bowl for when you grow old like Granddad."*

From that day forth the man made sure that his own father was eating at the same dinner table with the family as he realised the profound impression he was making on his own son.

Children do what you do, not what you say. You may think you are getting through to them (with some amazing speeches), but trust me, you have got to 'walk the talk' for them to truly understand and take heed, so lead by example.

*Respect peoples time –
don't be late!*

29

Blue sky time

*Try a bit of 'blue-sky' time in the morning before you
start your day.*

Watch the world go by.

Every morning, no matter where I am, whoever I am seeing, whatever
I am doing, I always get myself a coffee and go sit for 10 minutes in a
public space, whether it is busy or quiet, and watch the world go by.

This has been my fix each morning - it really has been just what the
doctor ordered - I love it!

This simple activity helps ground me for the day ahead and helps me
think better. Alternatively, you can get up at 5am in the morning and
meditate, do some yoga, or engage yourself in some other activity that

sets you up for the day. My option is not so strenuous, it is simple and effective. This may not work for you, but you must establish what does. Take some time out for yourself before you start your day.

In case you feel your day is *so* busy that you can't spare a few moments then that is fine too, there will come a day when you will have plenty of time on your hands. Read the title!

Reduce the amount of processed foods that go into your body.

30

Family peace conference

A family conference once in a while is no bad thing.

Talk to your family.

Some people may disagree, but I am of the view that having a positive, constructive discussion with your immediate family (or whatever your grouping may be) can strengthen your relationships. It needs to be an honest and open exchange about how each of you feel. The debate must allow people in the group to comment on how they can help each other.

Your family and friends teach you things about yourself all the time, be it your kids, your partner, your siblings or your parents. Whether or not you accept and embrace their opinions is entirely up to you.

Whether you act on it or not, is also a choice only you can make.

We all have our blind spots, and usually it is our nearest and dearest that are in the best position to see what we are unable to see ourselves. We do at times go through years in a relationship, completely unaware that we may be upsetting someone by acting in a certain way, even if we are not doing it maliciously. Instead of ignoring the issue addressing it is a lot easier and will cause a lot less destruction to the relationship going forward. Listening to concerns from your loved ones can be a real eye-opener, and when you have done it, you will wish you'd had the conversation earlier.

The idea is not to get too deep and fixated on particular issues - you will never find a resolution, and will end up going round in circles. This is not the objective behind the exercise.

However, it is very important that there are some **rules of engagement** in the conversation, which everyone must adhere to before you begin which are as follows:

1. There is no right or wrong in this discussion - you are not in a court of law.

2. If you have made a good point, don't get over excited or show off about it. Likewise if you are on the back end of a good point then don't get deflated by it either. View it as a positive that someone has been able to identify something about you which will help improve you as a person.

3. Don't interrupt any member, and only speak when they have finished what they are saying.

4. Don't raise your voice to speak over someone else.

5. If someone is getting emotional, let them finish and then try and bring down the tone, volume and emotion to a neutral level without sounding condescending.

6. If you can, keep sarcasm at bay.

7. Don't mimic another person in terms of their actions or how they express themselves.

8. Going forward, try and draw practical conclusions. The idea behind the exercise is not a blame game. If it looks more like an inquisition or personal vendetta, you will scare them off from sitting down again in the future.

9. Don't dig too deep into someone's history, and don't repeat previously discussed issues and arguments, unless they are relevant to the current discussion because then it becomes a jury trial. This is not constructive and ends up being a complete waste of time and energy. If there are deep-rooted issues that never seem to get resolved, no matter how many conferences you hold, then it is time to call in the experts to help you resolve them.

10. No hidden agendas please.

11. Don't use personal attacks to throw back at the person the minute they have had their say.

12. You need to listen carefully, absorb, analyse and weigh up why that person is expressing a certain view. Everyone is entitled to an opinion, whether it is right or wrong. Don't try and catch them out on a play of words - if you get the general gist of what they are saying then leave it at that! Don't take the discussion off-topic, stay focused and deal with the issues at hand.

13. It has to be an open, honest and constructive discussion, which will have positive and constructive criticism.

14. All mobile phones (or electronic devices) to be turned off. (As an aside, whenever you all go out as a family for breakfast/lunch/dinner, you should all place your mobile phones in the middle of the table, where no one can use them until you are finished. The first person to reach for the phone gets fined and has to pay for the meal!)

Remember the objective behind this exercise is to continually strengthen your relationships with those people that matter the most in your life.

Warning: It's not, I repeat *not* about opening a humongous can of worms and debating/arguing forever - it will be a complete waste of time and energy. If you cannot resolve issues within a few discussions then they can only be resolved through professional help.

Get yourself an annual MOT – a medical check-up; cholesterol, BP, heart rate, etc. A very good investment for this particular vehicle – trust me.

31

Parlez–vous français?

*Come on, at least try to make an attempt at learning
each other's language.*

Speak the same language.

You may never quite master it, but at least try and learn the key words
to be able to communicate effectively. In case you haven't realised, I'm
talking about the language you use in your relationships. You see, in
order for relationships to prosper you need to be speaking the same
language. When we travel to a foreign country, we take a pocket
translation book to help us communicate with the locals. In the same
way, this is required in a relationship so you can understand each
other. Being able to speak effectively will help strengthen your
relationships for sure.

Each of us has a unique way of communicating, but often the communication styles clash, as what we think we are saying to the other party, is not how they are hearing it. Therefore, rather than trying to change that person, adapt the way in which *you* communicate. Build a willingness to learn into your repertoire and be able to talk at different levels and in different ways.

I know it is an obvious point, but you will be surprised how many people ignorantly continue speaking in their own language without realising that the receiving party can't understand a word they are saying.

The best way to find out whether your form of communication is working is by following these short steps:

1. Get a piece of paper and draw a small circle in the middle of the paper and then write down the word **ME** in it.

2. Write down all the names of your *First Inner Family Tier* (FIFT) around your **ME** circle. These people include your partner, children, parents, brothers, sisters and grandparents.

3. Draw a circle around each of the *FIFT* names.

4. Draw a straight line from the **ME** circle to each of the *FIFT* names, connecting each one directly to the **ME**. So, if there are 12 people in your *FIFT* then draw 12 lines out from your **ME** circle.

5. Think of names that fit into your *Second Inner Tier (SIT)* circle. This includes your close friends, your In-Laws and people who have been very close to you over the years through blood, partnership or friendship. N.B. *The people you write down in*

this tier are who you have been connected to throughout your life, regardless of whether or not you share a good relationship with them, but outside of your partner, parents, children, brothers and sisters, they're the next closest connected.

6. Carry out the same process that you used for your *FIFT* names, however, place the SIT names slightly further out from the **ME** circle.

7. Grade each relationship as good (green), neutral (amber) or not so good (red), by colouring each circle accordingly.

N.B. In terms of defining good, neutral, or not so good, try the "Oh what a surprise, look who has come to visit us, dear" test.

If you are genuinely happy when you know who it is – that's green.
If you feel indifferent about your visitor – that's amber.
If you would rather not have seen the guest/visitor – then that's red.

Now the key point here is that the common denominator in the graph is the ME circle and if the chart is full of green, or over 70%, well done, this is a positive indicator of healthy relationships. If green is not the major colour, then you need to review why. These people are meant to be the closest relationships in your world, and if the major colour is amber or red, then you need to fix something that appears not to be working very well.

You may use the argument that all the people filed under red are all the same, and that they are the real problem, and they don't understand you, in which case, at the very least, try and get the relationship out of the red (bad status) and into the amber (neutral). This way, you needn't carry their negativity around with you, and you will have neutralised the relationship.

Turning negative relationships into neutral ones can make a positive difference in your life. A lot of people carry their bad relationships like a heavy bag on their shoulders, not realising that it weighs them down daily, eventually speeding up the ageing process and jading your perception of life.

This doesn't mean that the relationships that go from bad to neutral need to be fake or a farce, just that you have taken steps to remove the negativity.

Here is an example of what your circles may look like;

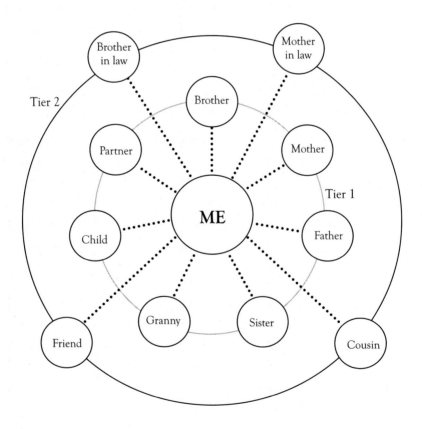

Eat only up to 75% of your capacity.

32

Play, rewind and pause – press play

Try if you can, to stop pressing the rewind button, as it slows down
what could be a great movie inspired by a true-life story.

"If only..."

The reality is that we spend too much time allowing our past to affect our everyday present. *"If only I had done that or this, I would not be here today; if only he had not said that, I would not feel this way or have acted in the way that I did; if only, if only, if only..."*

The past is exactly that – it has passed! Constantly revisiting events that are now behind you is akin to rewinding a DVD to a scene that you have already viewed; it takes up valuable time that could be used in a much more constructive manner. As a society, we spend too much time dwelling on the past and allowing it to affect our present (which is a bad investment of time), when we should be using our present to affect our future (which is a good investment of our time).

Draw wisdom from your past, and move forward by preserving what was good, this optimism is what should drive you.

Incidentally, on a seperate but equally important point, this particular DVD player of yours has no remote control, you need to get up and press play yourself!

Be yourself, because those that mind don't matter, and those that matter don't mind.

33

The amazing healing qualities of time

All the words, people, love, comfort and support in the world will never come close to the healing qualities that time provides.

Let time take its course.

It is the one thing that can make a difference to your life. If you respect time, then let time take its course. Only time fully respects how great love is, how great 'friendship' is and how great you and those around you are. Time ultimately reveals the truth.

One of my favourite stories about the value of time is about an island whose inhabitants consisted of many emotions. This island was sinking fast, and all the emotions had to leave to avoid drowning. Almost everyone got into their own boats to leave, apart from LOVE.

LOVE searched for someone who could help him leave the island. LOVE first asked ANGRY whether he could join his boat but the reply was *"I'm too angry to let anyone into my boat."* LOVE approached SADNESS to see if he had room in his boat. The response was, *"I'm too sad and need to be left alone."* LOVE approached GREEDY, but he refused too as he was busy taking all his possessions and couldn't make room for LOVE.

LOVE sat on the island whilst everyone made a hasty exit, when suddenly an elder, dressed in a dark cloak with his face hidden came over. Without saying a word, the elder summoned LOVE to an empty boat in which he sat himself, and rowed LOVE to safety. He helped him onto dry land, and quietly left without having said a word throughout the whole journey. LOVE was intrigued to find out who had helped him, but no one knew the answer until he came across another elder – WISDOM. When he asked WISDOM who the other elder was, he replied, *"the person who brought you here was TIME."* *"Why"*, asked LOVE, *"did TIME help me?"* WISDOM answered, *"Because only TIME truly appreciates how great LOVE really is."*

It's never too late to educate yourself.

34

The three faces

*Contrary to popular opinion (and science), every
person possesses three separate faces.*

This is my theory:

<u>First Face</u>

This is the face you present to the world, your family, your friends and
to the wider community. It is the face you want the world to see and
define who you are. It comes in different variations depending on who
you're dealing with, but it is what you essentially project outwardly.

<u>Second Face</u>

This is the face that you keep hidden, and exists between 'yourself'
and you. It is the person you believe you are. You can discover this

face by talking to yourself in a mirror, whilst alone (this is not a vanity exercise). You will find that there are one or two things in your life that you would prefer to keep to yourself. It may be something minor, but it is very rare that you will be 100% open to the world.

Third Face

This is the face that represents who you REALLY are, who even you may not know. It is the face that comes out in emergency situations when you don't have time to think, but you have to react spontaneously. It expresses itself through unique body language which forms part of your DNA that you simply cannot disguise. This face is void of any filters and is defined by your instinct – it represents the core of who you are.

Ideally all three faces should be similarly aligned, akin to having one face that actually represents you. Believe it or not in order to reach this state, you must first establish who face three is. When you achieve this, you will harmonise your mind and soul, creating a much more positive environment within which to live your life.

Remember you want the label on the outside to accurately reflect what's on the inside.

Do not overdo it on the toothpaste /shampoo.

35

Win yourself and you will win the world

Before you can achieve your aspirations and goals, you need to have a profound understanding of yourself.

What makes you, you?

Take some time to understand what makes you tick, what turns you off, what makes you angry, what makes you jealous, what makes you happy, what inspires you and what drives you.

Confucius once said, *"real knowledge is to know the extent of one's own ignorance."*

As you become more self-aware, you will be able to put some control systems in place, which will result in you becoming a lot more complete in your everyday life. Think of it akin to stripping a car engine and putting it back together in such a way that it allows the car to achieve double the output whilst consuming only half the energy.

By achieving a greater understanding, you will become a lot more real in your relationships as opposed to trying to appease others and become someone they want you to be. That is never a good thing, whichever way you look at it.

I often tell people about the story of the Emperor who wanted to take over the world. He invaded India with an army of a million soldiers, who made the ground shake beneath them as they marched. One day the Emperor came across an Indian Yogi sitting by a tree soaking up the sun. It intrigued him how this man was sitting undisturbed by the commotion. The Emperor got off his horse and stood in front of this man and asked him *"Are you not worried that your country is being invaded?"* the man replied *"No! What are you going to do next, once you have taken this country?"* The Emperor replied *"I will invade the next one after this."* The Yogi then questioned, *"So once you have taken over all the countries, what next?"* The Emperor then thought for a moment, and answered *"I will relax and take it easy."* The Yogi then responded, *"That is exactly what I'm doing right now, but I don't need to take over the world to do it."* He then kindly asked the Emperor to step out of the way, as he was blocking the suns rays. The Emperor decided to turn back his army and return to his country.

Although this story sends out a similar message to that of the Mexican fisherman, the point here is that some of us in our life try to win over the world when really we need to win ourselves first.

Don't bite your nails (trust me – it's a very bad look)!

36

Ego, meet humility – arrogance, meet wisdom

Don't make ego or arrogance your drivers,
control and steer them on an even keel.

The virtues of humility.

Once you appreciate the virtues of humility, you unlock the secret to life, which combined with intelligence can be a supreme combination!

Showing humility doesn't mean you are a doormat, instead bringing it into your life, business and relationships, will help you better understand people and situations, as it steers you clear of aggression, arrogance and sarcasm.

Imagine two cardboard boxes, one filled with ego and arrogance, and the other filled with humility and wisdom. In my eyes, the first represents a seductive, large, garish but empty box. The latter represents a simple, beautiful, yet understated one that is filled with many hidden treasures.

If you learn to listen more than you speak, you will be amazed at how much you can learn from people from all walks of life, be they a king or a common man.

The world does not just revolve around you – remember that!

*Take the juice out of life
before life takes the
juice out of you!

37

Box clever

"Remember, living in favourable and unfavourable situations is a part of life, but smiling in all those situations is the art of life." ~ *Source unknown*

Life is like a boxing ring.

Life is a bit like a boxing ring; you can fight the fight in one of two ways. You can go into battle with sheer brawn, knowing that you are going the distance. In the end, you may well be the successor, but you will have certainly given and taken some heavy knocks. You will be completely exhausted, and your body will take a while to recover until your next fight.

Then, there is a second way; those who box clever. They practise, they research their opponent, they understand their own body, and they have a strategy in mind. These people don't expect to be in the ring for more than two to three rounds; they box smart, they're quick on their feet, they know their opponents weak spots, and they place their punches inch-perfect and then back off.

Within three rounds, they knock out their opponent, and still have energy, ready for the next fight. Always remember that whatever situation you find yourself in, refrain from going in all guns blazing – think first, think wisely and then act!

Always box clever – it is the smart way forward.

The golden law of nature – what goes around comes around... look after your old!

38

It's not the place, it's the people

For over 25 years I have always made the time at least once a week, to meet up with my brothers and friends, and to share and catch up on the week's highs and lows.

I have been to some of the most wonderful venues in the world;

I have dined with the best and eaten at amazing restaurants the world over, but do you know what? As strange as it may sound, for me, nothing beats eating and drinking in a snooker hall in West London with the people I love.

Many of the people that I share this time with, I have shared my childhood and youth with. We all understand each other's sense of humour, share the same body language and joke naturally. No one needs to impress, no one needs to take the lead, we are all one. I am blessed to experience this environment on a regular basis.

It may not be a five-star hotel, but it is a place where I completely connect with the company I am in. It's the people, and not the place, that makes all the difference.

On a separate yet equally important note, through the years I did miss out on sitting around the table for dinner with my immediate family. I made other issues in my life more of a priority than this, and I am only now coming to realise that this should have been at the top of my list. The massive benefits one gets from this are obvious; it gives you the time to talk to your partner and your children, to really find out about their day, and give them the guidance they may be seeking. Sometimes, without realising it we can all be deprived of this treasure. It keeps you engaged with the trials and tribulations that the family experiences throughout the week, and I am fortunate that my wife always gives this the upmost importance.

Once again, it is the important people in life you need to find time for, the place doesn't matter. Try and make the time to connect more regularly with whoever it is in your life that you feel a deep connection with, those who can share your experiences without judgement.

Every now and then, make a visit (with your kids) to a care home for the elderly – just to say hello and find out how the residents are. You have no idea how much joy you will bring.

39

What is the true test when measuring your success?

Success is best measured not by the value of your bank balance,
but by the balance you have achieved in your life.

Investing in the wrong commodity.

A very dear friend of mine, the godfather to my youngest daughter as well as my father-in-law, have always given me their time and wisdom throughout the years. Their philosophy has been simple; we should use the spirit level of life to properly measure our success and to constantly review all that we set out to do, and make sure it is in balance with the environment we have created around us. They have most certainly been the spirit level to my life.

A lovely story to illustrate this relates to my father's 80th birthday, when all fifteen grandchildren got up on to the stage and spoke proudly about their grandfather's journey from birth to where he was now, and the contribution he had made to the lives of others. All his children spoke proudly of what their father meant to them. Then a gentleman spoke out and announced to several hundred close guests, *"I read the 'Times Rich List' this week and was surprised not to see Mr. Ajit Singh Rai's name on it."*

Now everyone knew that my father was not a financially rich man, and they thought this man was simply making fun. He went on to say, *"Any man who has all his grandchildren and children standing together as one, speaking so proudly and lovingly of him is, in my eyes, the richest man in the world."*

Many of us believe success is driven through the accumulation of wealth, so we all work hard to try and achieve a certain level of economic security. The problem is that when we've reached our requirement, we then strive for more, and start to acquire certain luxury goods that we feel will enhance the quality of our lives. Some of us buy these on credit, even when we can't afford them. They don't actually increase the quality of our lives but reduce it, as they make us a hostage to fortune as we have to keep working to pay for them. This is where our relationships suffer as we are investing in the wrong commodity. The irony is that often these purchases limit human interaction.

We must learn to stop and think about what we are doing, why we are doing it and who we are doing it for, before it is too late. Trust me, you are all losing out on valuable quality time with each other if you are investing in the wrong commodity, which ultimately takes time away from the very people you should be spending it with.

The most powerful words I heard from my father when I was young were, *that a man can always make money but money can never make a man!*

So true!

In space there is togetherness.

40

Character over gifting

Everyone wants to ensure that their children are provided with the best education and are given the best opportunities in order to excel in their chosen field, but we need to question if is this the only education they require?

Experiences of life.

Some of us fail in our inability to give our next generation a full and rounded education. This comes through the practical experiences of life; growing up, being able to deal with the rough and the smooth, and acquiring emotional intelligence and understanding so that they can handle situations when they arise. No amount of academic education can prepare our children for the real world, and youngsters who have been mollycoddled will suffer when faced with harsh realities. Additionally, if we view life as an education then surely it is more than academia, there are sports, arts, faith and human relations... the list is endless. The central pivot for all these attributes, that we so want to enrich our children's lives with, is balance.

My view is that a child who is exposed to the street markets, and observes and interacts with the characters that go through them in their daily lives is far better equipped to deal with the world, than those who have been wrapped up in cotton wool throughout their formative years.

It is the character of a child that always shines through, and is shaped by their colourful experiences which they encounter over time.

*Take a 15 minute nap
in the afternoon.*

41

The best anti-ageing product

I call it the 'Benjamin Button' potion – someone who gains their youth as each year passes.

Thinking positively.

The effect that our thoughts and general attitude can have on our ageing process is immense. Coupled with a healthier regime, a positive mind can make you look and feel younger – try it!

If it doesn't work, you can have your money back, but no cheating.

Aim for the 70% rule and you will not look back. I can't speak highly enough of the benefits of positive thinking. Give it a chance, plant it inside you and don't suffocate it; it creates possibilities that you could only dream of, as long as you take your daily dose.

Trust me, I know – my 115 year old grandmother was a great example.

Treat your house as a home, not your home as a house.

42

Say it before it's too late, while you still can

Don't leave it too late, as you may well regret it!

Say it today...

I have come across a number of people who say, *"I wish I could have told my parents/partner/children how I really felt about them rather than living day-to-day as if they didn't matter."* Well, your parents normally leave this world before you do, your partner may feel that there is little point in continuing your relationship if you don't communicate with them and your children will flee the nest to pursue their own lives if they feel like a piece of furniture. Shame.

While you still can, share and express what is in your heart with those nearest to you. If you don't, you will regret it later. At the very least please try and take time out for yourself and give some serious thought to how you feel about the people you love.

The time you invest into those that you love is invaluable, you may never get the opportunity, so do it now while you still can.

Don't get suckered into a green chilli eating competition – you will regret it in the morning!

43

The key elements to a meaningful life

A wonderful person I met many years ago, called Bonnie Katsumoto expressed her thoughts on what a meaningful life meant to her, for which I'm grateful;

To talk softly
To breathe deeply
To dress smartly
To work patiently
To behave decently
To save regularly
To eat sensibly
To sleep sufficiently
To act fearlessly
To think creatively
To earn honestly
To spend intelligently

Believe in yourself, you *are the one constant throughout your life, and the only one you can rely on.*

44

One's nature and one's habit

Two different beasts – one is what you are stuck with,
like it or not, the other is created and can be changed.

The Scorpion and the Turtle.

Nature is best explained through the story of the Scorpion and the Turtle.

An island was sinking, and as the Scorpion couldn't swim, he asked the turtle for a lift on his back. The Turtle exclaimed, *"Are you mad? You'll kill me".* The Scorpion replied, *"Are you mad? If I kill you, we both die."* The Turtle reflected and thought the Scorpion made a valid point. So the Turtle decided to take him on his back across to dry land. Half way across, the Scorpion stung the Turtle. The turtle looked back as he was drowning and asked, *"Why? Now, we will both die."*

The Scorpion looked back and said, *"I'm sorry, I don't know why I did it, it is just in my nature, and I can't help myself."*

When educating yourself, you need to identify what your bad habits and negative traits are. In order to establish which is which, you need to go back in time and retrace your childhood, your teenage years and where you are today. You'll be able to tell the difference between the bad habits you've picked up along the way and the natural negative traits you've been carrying with you throughout your life. We all know that habits can be changed, but one's nature can't, so try and control those negative traits as best you can.

* *Remember that sadness is part of our happiness – we should learn from it!*

45

The orchard of life

Your flowers have been well taken care of, but do you really want them to flourish in a desert?

Look after the orchard of life.

I believe we all have a duty of care towards the wellbeing of the next generation, not just environmentally, but mentally, physically and spiritually. While most of us genuinely try to achieve this within our own households, we sometimes neglect our responsibilities to those in the wider community. This is not to say that you should act superior by telling them how they ought to be living their lives. Rather, this is about us taking responsibility to help others in a positive, humble and intelligent way when we can see things are not going well.

Often, when confronted with another person's problem, our first reaction is *"it is not my problem."* Well, I am afraid when things turn up at your doorstep, it becomes your problem. At the very least, we need to start applying ourselves to solving it, otherwise we effectively disown the issue, hoping that someone else will come in and sort it out. We need to start thinking about society as a collective, who can work together to improve the wellbeing of those around us. If we all start thinking this way, we will inevitably create a better community.

Teaching our next generation the fundamental values of respect, tolerance, love and understanding is a good starting point. These four values don't require a religious order or dictum to be bestowed upon us, but just a bit of common sense and courage. If you can't help, then try and find someone who can – don't ignore it.

When you truly love life and people, you start a ripple effect that flows through society and changes the world for the better. Let's start with the next generation!

The other day, something happened that made me smile (while I was putting the final touches to these thoughts). My youngest daughter had been reading a book about Aboriginal life. She left a note next to my laptop, which reads as follows

"I think children need to read about these kind of things because it teaches them what life is about. Many don't even know what hardship is because they are too into TV, video games, phones, etc. We need to teach them these better ways."

I understood where she was going with this!!

I have a dream of my own, which if I may, I would like to share with you. About nine years ago, I had a 'light bulb' moment after reading my first life awareness book. (I've only read two to date.) About 20% of it was marketing and PR-heavy, but the rest was pure gold. I could not wait to share some of the ideas I had read with family and friends and others, but how was I going to do this? The concept of *'The Orchard of Life'* was born. The idea is to create a park which would be designed in the shape of a tree. The main route into this park would be through the trunk – the 'Path of Life', then it would fork with the 'Path of Relationships' to the left and the 'Path of Health' to the right. Further up you would have the 'Path of Belief' and the 'Path of Environment'. The idea is, that within this park, people would learn about ancient medicine, arts, exercise, recreation, history, philosophy from around the world. Every tree lining these paths would have a value, a virtue, or express an emotion that each of us experiences every day.

This park project would provide a sanctuary for people to be inspired and educated, not only by the past but enough to motivate them to live a more uplifting and progressive life.

I believe in today's modern world the fabric of family values and moral ethics has been weakened, but hopefully this *Orchard of Life* will help to reverse it or at least slow it down.

For me, these words sum up my idea of *'The Orchard of Life'* project; *"The true meaning of life is to plant trees under whose shade you don't expect to sit."* ~ **A Greek proverb**.

Stop pretending, stop appeasing – there's nothing wrong with you just being you. ✳

46

Forgiveness – a beautiful gift you give to yourself

It never fails to amaze me how unforgiving we can be at times. We sometimes lack the gift of tolerance, make judgements too hastily, and look for someone to blame too quickly.

The gift of forgiveness.

When you practise the gift of forgiveness, it is usually more for your benefit than for the person you are forgiving. It helps take away the feelings of anger and negativity, and passes those feelings over to a new custodian to deal with (the person you have just forgiven).

You have a life to live, and you may as well get on with living it without hauling resentment and revenge around with you, like a mule weighed down with its load. Let it go.

Try not to sanitise everything! A little bit of dirt now and then helps build up the immune system.

47

The 14-year life certificate

This is my gift to you; a 14-year life certificate.

Where will you be in 14 years' time?

Many people have enjoyed their lives, are happy with their lot and don't need the 14-year life certificate. However, there are so many more who haven't. So often you come across people who say, *"If only I could have those years all over again, I would do things so differently now, as I have learnt from my mistakes."*

As you are reading this, please imagine yourself in 14 years time, and take a few minutes to think about where you will be. If you base your prediction on your history, you will not be too far from the truth. By history, I mean the way and the manner in which you have lived your life so far, and how things have worked out for you. Think about the state of all your previous and current relationships, and the type of person you think you have become today, with an honest assessment of your strengths and weaknesses. Bring all this information together, follow the trajectory through and you will have a pretty decent idea of what to expect 14 years from now.

Let me tell you how quickly 14 years will fly by my friend. It was only yesterday (or maybe the day before) that we were celebrating the turn of the millennium – but we are now 14 years on (2013/2014) and you are probably saying to yourself right now, "*It's true, hasn't time flown by!*"

If you are content with what you see now and whom you will see in 14 years' time, then well done and keep going. If what you see in your future makes you feel somewhat anxious and apprehensive, then please read on.

Firstly, please close your eyes and take yourself to that age, look and place yourself where you think you are likely to be in 14 years from now and keep that thought.

Now, the second step is for you to make a request:

"*Jim, I read that passage of yours 14 years ago, could I please ask you to give me back those years – could you turn the clock back? I missed so much time with my children when they were growing up, and now they hardly know me. My parents have both died, and I did not get to spend enough time with them. I neglected my brothers and sisters, whom I have not spoken to for years as I have been so busy, and most importantly, my partner, to whom I paid no attention, has now left me.*"

Well, it must be your lucky day – I am going to give you your 14 years back starting right now, but I would ask just one thing of you – this time around, please don't waste it!

Trust me, if you are one of those people who feel that there are positive changes that can be made in your life, your outlook, and your attitude, then you literally can change it *today* if you really want to. Money, cars, and homes are made of paper, metal and bricks – they can never give you back the love you will get from real, genuine and strong relationships – the process is simple and will be so incredibly rewarding. Please make the right investment in your future.

Don't look at this 14-year life certificate as just another chapter, or clever idea – I have seen too many people who have lived their lives with money in the bank but their relationships lying in the bottom of a dark pit. You only realise these things when they are gone.

Give your life the time, reflection and make the adjustments it needs, so you enjoy the dividends here and now. Your dividends will certainly grow and give you the best rate of return.

Even Ebenezer saw the light in the end!

Remember, we are who we choose to be.

47 years and 47 lessons

So where have all these thoughts come from, you may ask?

They have come together from years of invaluable experience; meeting people from all walks of life, from my faith and my respect for its philosophy of equality, from the teachings of our elders and most importantly from my personal circumstances, as these were written during a period of my life which was certainly challenging and which helped catapult and crystallise these experiences onto these pages. I am just grateful that I finally made time for some quiet reflection on the direction ahead.

And life - what has it taught me so far?

In my world, it matters not which religion you practice or which background or culture you are from, what matters ultimately, is your respect for yourself and your relationships. If there is one thing for sure, it is this that we are all in our own individual carriages on this train journey. This train will never stop moving throughout time whether you are on it or not.

So, whilst in my carriage...

I have stopped at 47 different stations and with a bit of luck, will stop at a few more. I have enjoyed the ride so far, but can't help but think that at times, I have been sleeping for way too long during my journey.

Whilst in my carriage...

I have come to understand that this particular train will not be making a return trip, as the other two passengers with whom I boarded, (my parents) only purchased a one way ticket.

Whilst in my carriage...

I will continue to make the most of my time to get to know and value each of my fellow passengers, as I have no idea how long they will stay on board.

Whilst in my carriage...

I have had the chance to reflect on my experiences and learnt that it is important to grow wise before you grow old: I have learnt that time waits for no one and is on a course of its own; I have learnt that relationships are the only real thing we have in our lives, everything else is just a distraction; I have learnt that real and lasting charity is teaching a man to fish and not just providing a fish for the day; I have learnt that we have a responsibility for the wellbeing of others, our young and old; I have learnt that the choices I have made along the way are now behind me - it is time to look ahead. Most importantly, I have learnt to believe in myself, after all, we are who we choose to be, we just need to see that for ourselves.

And, whilst you are in my carriage...

I have one final request (I promise); should you ever need support, someone to talk to, a shoulder to cry on, a friend to rely on, then do please use this companion to motivate and uplift yourself.

Please take good care of yourself.

And above all else, have a safe and happy journey my friend!

About the author

Jim Rai grew up in a vibrant, multicultural neighbourhood in West London.

He spent the majority of his youth helping to run the family business, but soon realised that the only way 'out and up' was through education. After meeting his partner in 1986, he was more determined than ever to stand on his own two feet and make a life for himself. He worked his way through university and law school and finally qualified as a lawyer. Having applied the same work ethic that he had learned as a young man, he climbed the legal ladder, achieving a partnership in a well-established London law firm in his early thirties. Ironically, when he finally arrived at the top of his career, he decided to walk away, as he realised that chasing the materialistic dream simply was not all it was made up to be. Rather than adding to the quality of his life or his relationships, the chase had taken him away from the people he loved and the very reason for his being. He was only there to maintain the lifestyle he had been accustomed to and that simply was not enough to make him feel complete and alive.

Having woken from his long slumber, Jim has now embarked on a new journey, the steps of which are contained in these 47 thoughts. His message is simple; *that true success lies not in your material possessions or wealth, but in the strength of the relationships you create and in making the most out of them in the brief time you are here. Keeping it simple is the key.*

Love and time have true value, as they are what survive long after you are gone.

Jim Rai is a motivational speaker, life coach, author and entrepreneur.

A note for the reader

I do hope that this will not be the last you will be hearing from me. '...and then you're dead!' is the first in a series of thoughts and reflections which will be entitled, 'The Orchard of Life Series' (TOOLS). I have always viewed life and the way we live it as akin to an orchard of trees;

Time. Oh how the wonder of trees tell a curious story about time!
  Bent scarred branches or vines running down like ageing jewels
Happy green leaves admire its majestic trunk with pride
  But the stormy winds do come along and the branches collide.
Elegant in its own dance no matter how hard life is
  Sway and glide as the challenges come sprinting with the breeze
Own that dance, raise your arms as high as your branches could
  Tiptoe in grand-plie and absorb the upbeat mood.
Raise your arms, raise your elegant branches
  And remember to reach out
Cry if need be, like sap oozing from a wounded bark
  Often tears must flow for light to glow in the dark.
Hope when all seems broken for the golden sun rays to peek out
  When the ground has dried up, the teardrops from heaven fall
All your leaves may have dropped, don't you think of giving up
  Your trunk may be battered, get up and don't stop.
Run as many cycles as you must through the orchard of life,
  Enjoy but one chance, one breath in this lifetime
Death is no stranger, an inescapable universal truth
  "Live and let live"- whatever your age embrace youth!
Ordinary are our lives, nothing as spectacular as trees
  Juice to quench your thirst and shade for the homeless birds
Food from fruits to feed the hungry, a playground for all sorts
  Where squirrels, cats and monkeys dangle in all kinds of sports!
Life is full of remarkable mysteries like the magic of a tree
  In its roots are its nutrients; they are values to you and me
Inimitable in its form, fearless in its might
  Yet warm in its love to all beings in desperate plight.
Find your shape like the tree that grows freely in the forest
  Plant good seeds in this modern jungle that is fraught with pain
Every fine growth brings a confident smile like angels unfurled
  To do good deeds, one huge dearth in this funny cruel world.

Acknowledgments

The author wishes to thank the following people for their belief in him and in their indispensable help:

Ajit Singh Rai, my father, in making this possible in the first place. Karnail Singh Bhatti, my father-in-law, who has always brought a sense of balance to my life and Antoni Ferri my mentor, who has over the years, given me nothing but his sincerity, love and wisdom for which I will be forever grateful. Bubs Rai, Mandy Mann, Dr Edith Lochli and Reinout Van Lennep as the main movers and shakers in bringing this book to life with their genuine and constructive guidance throughout. Jasan and Preet Bhatti who read the early drafts and offered their perspective as part of our next younger generation. Tom Cassidy for his continuous positivity and inspiration along with Parita Shah for her relentless networking support. Nik Gupta for his constructive and instinctive feedback. My children, who would dip in and out, offering insightful observations to their father, which helped keep my thoughts in perspective. Neeta Udhian, Manjit Mann, who put their BA English degrees to good use and helped polish up the finished product. Alexa Whitten, Lisa Blann, Anjna Raheja (and her team at Media Moguls), Raj Ghai, Ben Nolan, Will Burnett, Karen Lane and Charlotte Clisby, who believed in the message from day one and helped deliver these thoughts to you. Paul and Sofie Louca, who were tasked with taking the picture (I am grateful for all the technology used to make it look half presentable). The lovely couple from Limassol, Artemis and Chris, for allowing me to sit in their café for hours on end, providing me with a constant supply of caffeine.

And last but not least, my five year old son, Jovan Bhagat Singh, who was always hovering around me like a butterfly, making the odd left field comment, which constantly brought a smile to my face and helped remind me why this book was so important to write and share three centuries of timeless wisdom... and of course to the everlasting guidance and presence from up above.